Stand Strong

I PETER

<u>Mission Vision</u>

" biblical scholarship

" fellowship "

Active in community

Praise God - Follow Him

① Pre - learning reading
② study @ will
they even outside of the study
② Accountability

(Steward to the Grace of God)

New Community Bible Study Series

BILL HYBELS

WITH KEVIN & SHERRY HARNEY

New Community
KNOWING. LOVING. SERVING. CELEBRATING.

Stand
Strong

I PETER

GRAND RAPIDS, MICHIGAN 49530

ZONDERVAN™

1 Peter: Stand Strong
Copyright © 1999 by the Willow Creek Association

Requests for information should be addressed to:

Zondervan, *Grand Rapids, Michigan 49530*

ISBN: 0-310-22773-9

Interior design by Sherri Hoffman

Printed in the United States of America

01 02 03 04 05 /❖ EP/ 10 9 8 7 6 5 4

CONTENTS

New Community
BIBLE STUDY SERIES

God has created us for community. This need is built into the very fiber of our being, the DNA of our spirit. As Christians, our deepest desire is to see the truth of God's Word as it influences our relationship with others. We long for a dynamic encounter with God's Word, intimate closeness with His people, and radical transformation of our lives. But how can we accomplish those three difficult tasks?

The New Community Bible Study Series creates a place for all of this to happen. In-depth Bible study, community-building opportunities, and life-changing applications are all built into every session of this small group study series.

How to Build Community

How do we build a strong, healthy Christian community? The whole concept for this study grows out of a fundamental understanding of Christian community that is dynamic and transformational. We believe that Christians don't simply gather to exchange doctrinal affirmations. Rather, believers are called by God to get into each other's lives. We are family, for better or for worse, and we need to connect with each other.

Community is not built through sitting in the same building and singing the same songs. It is forged in the fires of life. When we know each other deeply—the good, the bad, and the ugly—community is experienced. Community grows when we learn to rejoice with one another, celebrating life. Roots grow deep when we know we are loved by others and are free to extend love to them as well. Finally, community deepens and is built when we commit to serve each other and let others serve us. This process of doing ministry and humbly receiving the ministry of others is critical for healthy community life.

Build Community Through Knowing and Being Known

We all long to know others deeply and to be fully known by them. Although we might run from this level of intimacy at times, we all want to have people in our lives who trust us enough to disclose the deep and tender parts of themselves. In turn, we want to reveal some of our feelings, expressing them freely to people we trust.

The first section of each of these six sessions creates a place for deep knowing and being known. Through serious reflection on the truth of Scripture, you will be invited to communicate parts of your heart and life with your small group members. You might even discover yourself opening parts of your heart that you have normally kept hidden. The Bible study and discussion questions do not encourage surface conversation. The only way to go deep in knowing others and being known by them is to dig deep, and this takes some work. Knowing others also takes trust—that you will honor each other and respect each other's confidences.

Build Community Through Celebrating and Being Celebrated

If you have not had a good blush recently, read a short book in the Bible called Song of Songs. It's a record of a bride and groom writing poetic and romantic love letters to each other. They are freely celebrating every conceivable aspect of each other's personality, character, and physical appearance. At one point the groom says, "You have made my heart beat fast with a single glance from your eyes." Song of Songs is a reckless celebration of life, love, and all that is good.

We need to recapture the joy and freedom of celebration. In each session your group will commit to celebrate together. Although there are many ways to express joy, we will let our expression of celebration come through prayer. In each session you will take time to come before the God of joy and celebrate who He is and what He is doing. You will also have opportunity to celebrate what God is doing in your life and the lives of those who are a part of your small group. You will become a community of affirmation, celebration, and joy through your prayer time together.

You will need to be sensitive during this time of prayer together. Not everyone feels comfortable praying with a group of people. Be aware that each person is starting at a different place in their freedom to pray in a group, and be patient. Seek to promote a warm and welcoming atmosphere where each person can stretch a little and learn what it means to be a community that celebrates with God in the center.

Build Community Through Loving and Being Loved

Unless we are exchanging deeply committed levels of love with a few people, we will die slowly on the inside. This is precisely why so many people feel almost nothing at all. If we don't learn to exchange love with family and friends, we will eventually grow numb and no longer believe love is even a possibility. This is not God's plan. He hungers for us to be loved and to give love to others. As a matter of fact, He wants this for us even more than we want it for ourselves.

Every session in this study will address the area of loving and being loved. You will be challenged, in your personal life and as a small group, to be intentional and consistent about building love relationships. You will get practical tools and be encouraged to set measurable goals for giving and receiving love.

Build Community Through Serving and Being Served

Community is about serving and humbly allowing others to serve you. The single most stirring example of this is recorded in John 13, where Jesus takes the position of the lowest servant and washes the feet of His followers. He gives them a powerful example and then calls them to follow. Servanthood is at the very core of community. To sustain deep relationships over a long period of time, there must be humility and a willingness to serve each other.

At the close of each session will be a clear challenge to servanthood. As a group, and as individual followers of Christ, you will discover that community is built through serving others. You will also find that your own small group members will grow in their ability to extend service to your life.

Bible Study Basics

To get the most out of this study, you will need to prepare and participate. Here are some guidelines to help you.

Preparing for the Study

1. If possible, even if you are not the leader, look over each session before you meet, read the Bible passages, and answer the questions. The more you are prepared, the more you will gain from the study.
2. Begin your preparation time with prayer. Ask God to help you understand the passage and apply it to your life.
3. A good modern translation, such as the New International Version, the New American Standard Bible, or the New Revised Standard Version, will give you the most help. Questions in this guide are based on the New International Version.
4. Read and reread the passages. You must know what the passage says before you can understand what it means and how it applies to you.
5. Write your answers in the spaces provided in the study guide. This will help you to participate more fully in the discussion, and will also help you personalize what you are learning.
6. Keep a Bible dictionary handy to look up unfamiliar words, names, or places.

Participating in the Study

1. Be willing to join in the discussion. The leader of the group will not be lecturing but will encourage people to discuss what they have learned in the passage. Plan to share what God has taught you during your preparation time.
2. Stick to the passages being studied. Base your answers on the verses being discussed rather than on outside authorities such as commentaries or your favorite author or speaker.

3. Try to be sensitive to the other members of the group. Listen attentively when they speak, and be affirming whenever you can. This will encourage more hesitant members of the group to participate.
4. Be careful not to dominate the discussion. By all means participate, but allow others to have equal time.
5. If you are a discussion leader or a participant who wants further insights, you will find additional comments in the Leader's Notes at the back of this book.

1 Peter — Stand Strong

Standing in the Flood

Picture yourself standing in the flood plain of a rising river. The waters slowly creep higher and higher. The current grows faster and faster. You still have your footing, but you fear that, at any moment, your feet could slip and you will be washed downstream.

Your mailbox receives a steady stream of bills, but your bank account doesn't match your expenses . . . *the river rises.* Your schedule is out of control and your relationships are strained . . . *the current gains speed.* Pressures at work are mounting, and every morning you wake up with a knot in your stomach . . . *the ground beneath your feet begins to give way as the waters press against you.* You try to hold on, but you are not sure how long you can stay your ground.

Sound too familiar? Well, you're not alone. This was also the life story for many Christians in the first century. There were pressures, conflicts, and tensions everywhere. When Peter wrote to these followers of Christ, his words brought hope in the middle of a rising river of troubles. And you will find these words of Peter are just as powerful, relevant, and needed today as they were two thousand years ago. If you need strength to stand against the crosscurrent of life's troubles, the words of 1 Peter are for you!

Meeting Peter

Almost everyone knows Saint Peter. Even if a person did not grow up in or around the church, they still know him as the guy standing by the pearly gates when anyone tells a joke about heaven.

Peter was the leading man among the disciples of Jesus Christ. When the disciples are listed, he is usually the first one named. Even in the famous threesome of those who followed Jesus most closely he always comes first: Peter, James, and John.

Peter was the outspoken disciple. He was a man of action. Peter is remembered for walking on water with great faith and then sinking when fear took over. You always knew where Peter stood on an issue. He was quick to say exactly what he believed or feared. He was the one who made the great confession, "You are the Christ, the Son of the living God," and later he declared, "I don't know the man!" In the Garden of Gethsemane Peter rose up to defend Jesus and cut off the ear of the servant of the high priest, only to have Jesus rebuke him and heal the man. One moment Peter was solid as a rock, and the next he was as unstable as shifting sand.

A biography of Peter before Pentecost would read like many of our life stories. As a new believer Peter grew, fell, deepened as a disciple, struggled, totally surrendered his life, and then stumbled again. At times Peter was mature and stable. At other times he was discouraged and fearful.

After Pentecost and the coming of the Holy Spirit, however, Peter experienced radical transformation. He preached his first sermon, and three thousand people became followers of Christ. He performed healing miracles. He was threatened, beaten, flogged, and thrown in prison for preaching the gospel. Instead of quitting, he kept on preaching with boldness. Once, after being beaten for his faith, Peter said, "I rejoice that God would consider me worthy to be beaten in Jesus' name." The same Peter who had denied Jesus three times was now willing to suffer for Him . . . gladly!

Church history tells us that Peter was sentenced to die by crucifixion under the Emperor Nero, in about A.D. 64. Just before Peter was nailed to the cross, he was granted one final request. He asked to be crucified upside down. Reportedly, he said, "I don't even deserve to hang on a cross the way my Lord did."

The Reason for Writing

Near the end of his colorful life, Peter was moved by the Holy Spirit to write a letter to believers who found themselves scattered all over Asia Minor. These believers had been scattered by the persecutions brought about by Nero, the Roman emperor. After three days of fires in Rome, where much of the city burned, Nero needed a scapegoat. He used a very convenient target . . . the Christians. In an effort to appease the angry masses, Nero began to persecute the Christians, using beatings, floggings, and imprisonment.

With time, the persecutions escalated as Nero's need for blood led to tortures, burnings at the stake, crucifixions, and coliseum atrocities. Christians were killed for sport. The persecution started in Rome, but it spread throughout the entire Roman Empire. Pretty soon Christians were fair game for almost anyone. Chased, hunted, and running for their lives, Christians dispersed all over the Asian world. This was the situation followers of Christ faced when Peter wrote his first letter.

Things got so bad that many of the early Christians began living and hiding out in the catacombs, which were a series of tunnels underneath the city of Rome, originally designed to bury people. These tunnels had little caves on either side of the main passageways that would function as vaults for corpses. For years, many Christian refugees lived in these tombs.

Try to imagine a new follower of Christ and his family being chased out of their hometown because of their faith. All they had worked for, established, and accumulated in their lives was now gone. They were forced to leave their roots and flee for their lives. This is the situation Christ's followers were in when Peter wrote these words. They were a persecuted minority living on the run.

Stand Strong!

We all face times of struggle, pain, tension, and conflict. Peter offers great news for everyone who follows Christ. The storms of this life do not have to sweep you away, destroy your family, erode your business, or drown your hopes. God offers overcoming power to stand strong in the storms of life. My prayer is for you to grasp the hand of God in the midst of the storm and find His power to stand strong!

A Life of Hope

I PETER 1:1–21

It is 2:00 A.M. and you are deep asleep. You wake up to the sound of pounding on your front door. You jump out of bed and race for the door as you notice your two children standing in the hallway crying. Before you reach the door, it comes shattering in toward you.

Men with guns, lights in your eyes, screaming, and then . . . nothing! When you regain consciousness you realize hours have passed. Your wife is by your side, and so are your children. They are bandaging up the wound on your head with strips of cloth from your son's T-shirt. It is cold and damp. As your eyes begin to focus you see stars above.

"Why are we outside? What's happening?" you whisper.

With tears your wife says, "The government—they took everything! Our house, cars, clothes, food, money . . . everything! All because we are Christians."

In one day, your whole life has radically changed. You are now poor, persecuted, a target, an exile. You won't gather with your friends for church this Sunday. As a matter of fact, you don't even know where they are. You sit there with a numb mind and bruised body trying to grasp what has just happened to you and your family.

Can you imagine this horrific scenario? Many Christians in the first-century church did not have to imagine, they lived it. They ended up running for their lives and hiding in tombs just to stay alive.

Making the Connection

1. If you lived through a time of persecution like the one described above, what are two things you would miss from your old way of life?

   What are two things you have that no person, government, or time of persecution could take away from you?

Knowing and Being Known

Read 1 Peter 1:1–5

2. How could the words of Peter in these opening verses bring comfort and hope to people who had been driven from their homes and exiled to foreign lands?

3. God has offered a storehouse of treasures for all who follow Him. What are some of the treasures Peter highlights that can never be taken away?

How have you experienced one of these treasures in your own life over this past year?

4. God has promised a priceless inheritance that never perishes, spoils, or fades. How might this news have brought hope to Christ followers who were living in the catacombs?

How does the certainty of your heavenly inheritance help you through times of loss and struggle?

The Voices of the Martyrs

God you are with me
   and you can help me;
You were with me when I was taken,
   And you are with me now.
You strengthen me.

The God I serve is everywhere—
   In heaven and earth and the sea,
but he is above them all,
   For all live in him:
All were created by him,
   And by him only do they remain.

I will worship only the true God;
   You will I carry in my heart;
No one on earth shall be able to
   Separate me from you.

—Quirinus of Siscia
Arrested for his faith, tortured,
and executed by drowning, A.D. 308

There is but one king I know;
   It is He that I love and worship.
If I were to be killed a thousand times
   For my loyalty to him,
   I would still be his servant.
Christ is on my lips,
Christ is in my heart;
   No amount of suffering will take him from me.

—Genesius of Rome
Martyred by Diocletian in A.D. 285

Read 1 Peter 1:6–12

5. Peter describes some of the fruit that is born in our lives through times of trial. What grows in the life of a follower of Christ through times of struggle, loss, and trials? (vv. 6–9).

6. Tell your group members about a loss or time of struggle you have faced in the past year.

    How did you experience God's presence and work in your life through this time?

7. Peter promises that our trials can bring "praise, glory and honor" to Jesus Christ. How have you seen God receive praise through a time of trial and struggle?

A Grace Disguised

In his book, *A Grace Disguised* (Zondervan, 1996), Gerald Sittser addresses the reality of suffering, trials, and loss. His own loss came in the fall of 1991 when a drunk driver crossed into oncoming traffic and struck the van he was driving. In a fraction of a second, his life was changed forever. He watched his wife, mother, and daughter all die before his eyes. In the introduction of his book, Jerry writes:

> As I reflect on the story of my loss, I have learned that, though entirely unique (as all losses are), it is a manifestation of a universal experience. Sooner or later all people suffer loss, in little doses or big ones, suddenly or over time, privately or in public settings. Loss is as much a part of normal life as birth, for as surely as we are born into this world we suffer loss before we leave it.
>
> It is not, therefore, the experience of loss that becomes the defining moment in our lives. . . . It is how we respond to loss that matters. The response will largely determine the quality, the direction, and the impact of our lives.

Read 1 Peter 1:13–21

8. In verse 13 Peter has a big "Therefore." It is a radical call to right *attitude* and *action*. What are five attitudes or actions Peter calls us to incorporate into our lives (vv. 13–16)?

    •

    •

    •

    •

    •

Why are these attitudes and actions essential for an authentic Christian life?

9. How is God challenging you and growing you in one of these areas?

How can your group members encourage and pray for you in this area?

What Is It "There For?"

It has been said, "Every time you see the word *therefore* in the Bible, be sure to ask, 'What is it there for?'" Too often we look right past some very significant words in the Bible. The use of *therefore* sets the stage for what will follow. In this case, Peter is pulling together all he has said and is getting ready to call people to action. The word *therefore* at the beginning of this section is very significant . . . don't miss it!

10. How would you respond to one of these statements or questions in light of verses 18–21:

"I don't think followers of Christ should talk about the blood of Jesus and His suffering; this topic could be offensive to seekers who are investigating the claims of Christianity."

"I've always admired Jesus. I think He was a good man and a wonderful moral teacher. What I don't get is why Christians think His death two thousand years ago could actually impact people today."

"I don't know a lot about world religions, but they all seem pretty much the same. What is unique or different about the Christian faith?"

Celebrating and Being Celebrated

Take a couple of minutes as a group and list as many earthly treasures as you can. These are not "earthly" in any negative way; they are simply the material blessings of life. Thank God for all He has given you and celebrate His generous love.

Take another few minutes and talk about the heavenly treasures you have. These are things given by God that no one can take away. They are part of your inheritance package that will never fade, spoil, or perish.

Close your group with a time of prayer celebrating all God has provided for you.

Serving and Being Served

One of the ways God carries us through times of trial is on the shoulders of other Christ followers. In this session a number of your small group members told about a trial they are facing. Choose one person and commit yourself to do three things in the coming week:

1. Pray every day for this person.
2. Send them an encouraging note letting them know you are praying and that you share in their pain and time of trial.
3. Call this person and ask what you can do to serve and support them.

Loving and Being Loved

Often we value something in relationship to how much it costs us. After paying our mortgage bill month after month, year after year, we value our home. It is a huge investment! A new car can cost thousands or even tens of thousands of dollars. We pay our monthly bill, plus insurance, gas, and repair costs . . . you better believe we place a high value on our vehicle. The more something costs us, the more we value it!

If we want to know how much people matter to God, we simply have to ask, "What price has God paid to be in relationship with us?" The price paid reflects the value of the relationship. To get a window into the depth of God's love for us, memorize 1 Peter 1:18–19:

> *For you know that it was not with perishable things such as silver or gold that you were redeemed from the empty way of life handed down to you from your forefathers, but with the precious blood of Christ, a lamb without blemish or defect.*

In the coming days, reflect on the fact that God paid the ultimate price to show His love to you and each person in your life. How should this impact the way you view yourself and the people around you?

A Life of Love

I PETER 1:22–2:10

When a lawyer stands up to make a case in court, his goal is to marshal all the evidence that is in his favor. No lawyer expects to win a case with just one witness or one piece of evidence. The goal is to line up as many witnesses as possible. He brings in professionals who will give authoritative testimony that supports his case. He piles up as much physical evidence as he can find. He calls forward character witnesses and every other possible piece of evidence that might tip the scales in his favor. The more solid evidence he can bring, the better his chance of winning the case.

The Bible builds a strong case for many truths, but perhaps the most prominent theme in all of the Bible is love. The word *love* occurs over five hundred times in the Bible. Over and over again the words of the Bible strengthen the case for loving God and loving others. It all begins with an understanding of God's love for us, and then we discover God's call for us to love each other. Because people matter to God, they should matter to us. God loves people and calls us to do the same.

Imagine a lawyer coming to trial and being asked to build a biblical case for love. Here are just a handful of passages which could be used to argue the case:

Your love, O LORD, reaches to the heavens,
  your faithfulness to the skies.
Your righteousness is like the mighty mountains,
  your justice like the great deep.
O LORD, you preserve both man and beast.
How priceless is your unfailing love!
Both high and low among men
  find refuge in the shadow of your wings.

(Psalm 36:5–7)

25

Jesus said,

"A new command I give you: Love one another. As I have loved you, so you must love one another. By this all men will know that you are my disciples, if you love one another."

(John 13:34–35)

And now these three remain: faith, hope and love. But the greatest of these is love.

(1 Corinthians 13:13)

Dear friends, let us love one another, for love comes from God. Everyone who loves has been born of God and knows God. Whoever does not love does not know God, because God is love. This is how God showed his love among us: He sent his one and only Son into the world that we might live through him. This is love: not that we loved God, but that he loved us and sent his Son as an atoning sacrifice for our sins. Dear friends, since God so loved us, we also ought to love one another. No one has ever seen God; but if we love one another, God lives in us and his love is made complete in us.

(1 John 4:7–12)

Perhaps the most well-known verse in all of the Bible centers on this critical theme of love.

For God so loved the world that he gave his one and only Son, that whoever believes in him shall not perish but have eternal life.

(John 3:16)

Making the Connection

1.   Describe ways you experienced the love of God.

Love's Foundation

Peter's exhortation to love is rooted in the "before and after" of conversion: Since you have been purified, love one another, because you have been born again. The foundation for love that Peter builds on is that "you have purified yourselves by obeying the truth so that you have sincere love for your brothers." The result of obeying the truth was that they were ushered into the realm of brotherly love.

Almost redundantly, Peter exhorts his addressees to "love one another deeply, from the heart." The word *deeply* speaks of the effort required for that love, the depth of it for one another, and the duration of it (until the end).... Peter expects his churches to be filled with people who love one another, who give the other person the benefit of the doubt, and who reach out to others in the same love.

—Scot McKnight, *NIV Application Commentary on 1 Peter*
(Zondervan, 1996)

How has this experience affected your ability to extend love to others?

Knowing and Being Known

Read 1 Peter 1:22–2:3

2. In verse 22, Peter commands two things in a specific order. What are they?

3. Why is this order essential if we are going to live as healthy, loving followers of Christ?

    How is this order reflected in the Ten Commandments (Exodus 20:1–17)?

    Describe a time when you put loving others before loving God. What were some of the consequences?

4. According to verses 23–25, what is the reason for and source of our love for each other?

5. As Peter calls us to true love, he also reminds us of some of the attitudes and actions that can erode and destroy love among Christ's followers (2:1). Describe how you have seen one of the following attitudes or actions undermine love:

   • Malice
   • Deceit
   • Hypocrisy
   • Envy
   • Slander

6. According to verses 2–3, how can we rid ourselves of these evil attitudes or actions?

A Holy Priesthood

The great new truth Peter states here is the revelation that "through Jesus Christ," i.e., through his work on the cross, every Christian is part of a new priestly order. This truth of the "priesthood of all believers" was rediscovered and reemphasized during the Reformation. It means that every Christian has immediate access to God, that he serves God personally, that he ministers to others, and that he has something to give. It does not mean that each Christian has public gifts of preaching or teaching. In this verse Peter is stressing the reassuring fact that through Christ the believer is able to worship and serve God in a manner pleasing to him.

—*Expositor's Bible Commentary CD-ROM* (Zondervan)

Read 1 Peter 2:4–10

7. Peter describes the church as a building of living stones. What does this metaphor teach you about the church?

8. Who is one specific person (stone) in God's family who has helped to build you up?

   If this person were removed from your life today, what would you miss the most?

   What would the church lose if this person were removed from its structure?

9. In the Old Testament, only priests had access to the presence of God. Now, Peter declares with boldness that every follower of Christ is a priest (2:5 and 9). How did Peter's statement startle the first-century church?

Do you have the same access to God as a pastor or mission leader?

10. There were special honors for the priests. How can we show honor to each other as members of God's holy priesthood?

Celebrating and Being Celebrated

Take time as a small group to celebrate your giftedness and callings. Lift up prayers of praise for the gifts of each member of the group. Appreciate and enjoy the gifts of love and service you receive from each other. And ask God to further develop those gifts and make them fruitful.

31

Serving and Being Served

Peter is clear that we are all God's ministers, a holy priesthood. In many churches, the pastors are seen as the ones who *do* ministry, and church members are the ones who *receive* ministry. This can lead to an unhealthy imbalance in the church. Have a representative of your small group contact your pastor, or a member of your pastoral staff, and ask: "What could the members of our small group do to serve you in the coming month?" Then follow through on their answer. This will be more appreciated than you may ever know!

Loving and Being Loved

Find some way to communicate your love and appreciation to someone who has fortified and deepened your faith in God. Express gratitude to this fellow believer in a creative or surprising way.

A Life of Submission

I PETER 2:11–3:7

We live in a world where lives are coming apart. Nations are in turmoil, there is tension in the workplace, marriages are unraveling, and relationships are fractured. What I have discovered over the years is that this cycle of destruction is sinisterly slow. Relationships rarely blow apart; sadly, most people simply drift apart.

It is like the story of the frog in the kettle. It is said that if you drop a frog in a kettle of boiling water, it will hop out and jump away. However, if you put the same frog in a kettle with water at room temperature, he will stay in the water. If you then begin to heat up the water, the frog will stay in the kettle and not notice the slow increase in temperature. The frog will actually boil to death and never jump out of the pot.

This slow process of death has been experienced by nations, businesses, churches, friendships, and marriages. Slowly the temperature rises, the standards change, commitments erode, and before we know it, the water is boiling!

A Strategy of Submission

What is this thing called submission? Few subjects can cause more confusion or destruction than deficient teaching and lack of understanding of the subject of submission. Many people consider the word *submission* to be synonymous with weakness, cowardliness, and lack of conviction. This is deeply wrong!

One of the strongest drives in a human being is the incessant drive to get our own way and to control others. From our earliest years as children we cry out, "I want it my way!" Some people in management put it this way, "It's my way or the highway!" Even in the little things of life, we can stiffen our spine and demand our way.

Submission might be described as the courage to graciously allow something to go someone else's way instead of my way. It means to give deference to another, to willingly yield rights, agendas, and ego for the sake of building community. Submission does not equal mindless compliance. The Bible does not say that everything the government tells us to do is right and we should do it without thinking. It does not say everything your employer says is right and direct from the mouth of God. The Bible also does not say your spouse is always right. The Bible never calls us to throw judgment, discernment, feelings, or spiritual integrity out the window and become a puppet. God places no premium on ignorance.

But God does call us to a biblical spirit of submission. Every believer needs to develop an internal security and courage to set aside a personal agenda. From time to time, we all need to silence the cry, "My way!" for the sake of Jesus, family, another believer, our marriage, or our friendships. Sometimes we need to say, "Let's do it your way this time!"

Making the Connection

1. Give an example of how you have seen the "frog in the kettle" syndrome in one of the following areas:

   - As a marriage has come apart
   - As a friendship has slowly disintegrated
   - As a workplace has became a war zone
   - As a church has cut loose from its biblical moorings and been set adrift

Knowing and Being Known

Read 1 Peter 2:11–12

2. Peter called the early Christians "aliens" and "strangers." Why were these terms so appropriate for followers of Christ in the first century?

    How do the terms "alien" and "stranger" apply to your life as you follow Christ in the twenty-first century?

3. What does Peter call followers of Christ to do, and not to do, because of their status as aliens and strangers in this world?

The Greatest Example of Submission in History

Peter holds Jesus up as our ultimate example of submission. Even when it was painful beyond description, Jesus submitted His will to the will of the Father. This is portrayed for us clearly in the gospel of Matthew (26:36–45). Read these words slowly and reflect on Jesus' example of submission:

> Then Jesus went with his disciples to a place called Gethsemane, and he said to them, "Sit here while I go over there and pray." He took Peter and the two sons of Zebedee along with him, and he began to be sorrowful and troubled. Then he said to them, "My soul is overwhelmed with sorrow to the point of death. Stay here and keep watch with me."
>
> Going a little farther, he fell with his face to the ground and prayed, "My Father, if it is possible, may this cup be taken from me. Yet not as I will, but as you will."
>
> Then he returned to his disciples and found them sleeping. "Could you men not keep watch with me for one hour?" he asked Peter. "Watch and pray so that you will not fall into temptation. The spirit is willing, but the body is weak."
>
> He went away a second time and prayed, "My Father, if it is not possible for this cup to be taken away unless I drink it, may your will be done."
>
> When he came back, he again found them sleeping, because their eyes were heavy.
>
> So he left them and went away once more and prayed the third time, saying the same thing.
>
> Then he returned to the disciples and said to them, "Are you still sleeping and resting? Look, the hour is near, and the Son of Man is betrayed into the hands of sinners."

Read 1 Peter 2:13–25

4. In this passage, God calls us to have a willing and submissive spirit toward our government, our employer, and our spouse. What could happen in one of these areas of life if we became submissive and said, "Let's do it your way this time"?

5. Many people live with a fear of submission. How would you finish one of the statements below:

  - I'm afraid to be submissive to my boss because if I was ...
  - I'm afraid to be submissive to my spouse because if I was ...
  - I'm afraid to be submissive to the government because if I was ...

6. Peter is crystal clear that we are called to live in submission to the governing authorities (2:13–17). What should mature, Christ-honoring submission look like in our relationship to the government in one of these areas:

  - How we obey the law when we are driving a car
  - How we fill out our tax forms
  - How we speak when we are in court or a legal proceeding

7. Although it is not a perfect parallel, one of the best comparisons to submitting to your master in the first century is employment today (2:18–20). What should mature, Christ-honoring submission look like in our relationship to our employer in one of these areas:

   - How you conduct yourself when you are "on the clock" but no one is watching
   - How you use company supplies, equipment, phones, and other resources for personal reasons
   - How you speak of and treat your superiors in the workplace

8. In light of 1 Peter 2:21–25 and Matthew 26:36–45, how is Jesus our ultimate example of submission?

How can we apply the principle of submission to a situation in our own lives?

A Challenge to Husbands and Wives

In this passage the apostle Paul gives a charge to both wives and husbands. In each case there are three primary aspects of Paul's counsel. To wives he says:

- *Be submissive.* Peter calls wives to have a humble and submissive spirit with their husbands. There needs to be a willingness to say, "Let's do it your way this time."
- *Be pure.* Peter is specifically addressing women who have non-believing husbands, calling them to model purity and good deeds so that their husbands will see their example and be drawn to God. However, this also applies to all believers and Christlike relationships. God desires your purity to be so unwavering that it inspires others to live a pure and holy life (Ephesians 5:1–7, 21; 1 Corinthians 13).
- *Be beautiful.* This is not a call to outward attractiveness, but to genuine inner beauty. God is calling women to major on inner beauty and minor on outer beauty. One is clearly more important than the other.

To husbands he says:

- *Be considerate.* Her feelings, wants, and desires matter! Learn to know what she wants and take your turn saying, "Let's do it your way this time." A considerate husband does not demand his way, but longs to be deeply considerate of his wife's needs and wants, her hopes and dreams.
- *Live with your wife.* This is a call to do much more than simply share a house and a bed. Living with your wife means knowing her, listening to her, talking with her, laughing with her, and investing significant amounts of time in your marriage relationship. The truth is, more marriages erode than explode. There needs to be a deep commitment to being together.
- *Be respectful.* When Peter speaks of the woman as "the weaker partner" he is not addressing moral character or emotional strength. He is acknowledging that there is a general physical difference between men and women. Men are not to use their physical strength to take advantage in marriage. And Peter drives home the truth that men and women in Christ are "heirs" together of the "gracious gift of life." Mutual respect was a unique concept in the first century!

Read 1 Peter 3:1–7

9. How can husbands and wives:

- show love and respect for one another?
- develop a spirit of purity that will be plain for all to see?
- nurture an inner beauty?

Celebrating and Being Celebrated

Take time as a group to pray for God's power and presence to be experienced in:

- The lives of your local, state, national, and world leaders. Pray for leaders by name.
- The lives of your employers and those who are in leadership in your workplace.
- The lives of your family members, particularly the life of your spouse if you are married.

Serving and Being Served

One of the best ways you can serve your husband or wife is through knowing their needs and desires. Commit yourself to use some of the questions below to get to know your spouse's needs. Seek to identify a way to serve your spouse that would bring joy and honor to the relationship.

Here are some questions that might help you.

- What gives you the greatest fulfillment?
- What frustrates you more than anything?

- What qualifies as a romantic evening for you?
- What problems or obstacles could I help you with?
- What can I do on a regular basis to share the load of life with you?

Loving and Being Loved

Take time as a group to discuss one or two community or national leaders who are serving well. Write to them and communicate how much you appreciate what they do for others. Let them know that you thank God for their service.

A Life of Purpose

I PETER 3:8–4:6

Imagine walking through the mall and coming to a booth where a salesman is peddling bright orange life jackets. He is trying to gather a crowd with enthusiastic gestures and excitement in his voice. You pause more out of curiosity than interest in his product. He is carefully explaining the various properties of the life jacket. He tells about its flotation capacity, its unique harness system, its rating on how long it will keep a person afloat, its manufacturer's guarantee, and of course, its cost. You notice that about 99 percent of the people in the mall simply walk by with no sign of interest. Those who do pause seem more interested in his charismatic sales style than the actual life jacket he is trying to sell. No one seems very excited about buying a bright orange life jacket this particular day.

Now imagine you are on a cruise ship in the middle of the Atlantic ocean. The ship has just struck an uncharted reef, and water is gushing in through an enormous gash in the side of the boat. A young cabin boy is holding up that same orange life vest and, with a quaking, nervous voice, is telling a crowd of people about the various properties of this life-saving device. The young man does not have great communication skills, a charismatic personality, or a dynamic sales pitch. But each person is hanging on his every word.

What has changed? Why are people so interested in a plain, ordinary life jacket all of a sudden?

A life jacket can seem like an unnecessary accessory—until the boat starts sinking. A fire extinguisher hanging on a wall in a kitchen is hardly noticed—until a grease fire flares up. A job can feel like a burden—until you discover that your company is "downsizing" and that you no longer fit into their plans for a brighter corporate future. A Bible can be a table decoration in the living room—until a crisis hits a family and they need the comfort found within its pages. Many things in life are valued only when they are needed.

Making the Connection

1. Describe a time when something ordinary, plain, and accessible became essential in your life.

What brought about this dramatic change?

Knowing and Being Known

Read 1 Peter 3:8–17

2. Peter gives us some guidelines for living with a clear conscience. In 1 Peter 3:8–12 he gives direction to all followers of Christ. What does he call us to do?

What does he say we should not do?

Doing Time with Your Conscience

The article was entitled, "The Duties of a Bystander." It read, in part, "The crime is beyond exaggeration. Four men repeatedly raped a woman in a New Bedford, Massachusetts bar while a crowd of drinkers stood by. Last week a grand jury indicted the alleged rapists and two of the witnesses who reportedly encouraged the attack and helped hold the woman down on a pool table. But what about the others? Police say that no one came to the victim's aid."

Not only did no one help, but of those who left the bar during the two-hour attack, not one bothered to call the police. We might feel that these people had an ethical obligation to help the woman, or at least to call the police, but the article said they were under no legal obligation to do anything. Where strangers are involved, the criminal law did not recognize crimes of omission. Witnesses are not required to report crimes and will not be held accountable for their silence, the article reported.

One attorney quoted in the article gave an example of a baby slipping off a dock into three feet of water. All an onlooker would have to do is get their shoes wet to save the baby. Can this person stand there, do nothing, and not be guilty? According to the law at that time, yes!

The article ended by saying, "The witnesses in Big Dan's Tavern may not go to prison, but they will do time with their consciences."

3. Looking at the list above, how can following Peter's counsel help us live with a clean conscience?

4. According to verse 16, in what way should you "give the reason for the hope that you have"?

Why are these two qualities important to communicating your faith effectively?

Read 1 Peter 3:18–22

5. What was the condition of the world and human hearts in Noah's day? (Genesis 6:5–8).

How is our world today like the world of Noah's day?

One with Christ

Faith unites the soul with Christ as a bride is united with her bride-groom. As Paul teaches us, Christ and the soul become one flesh by this mystery (Ephesians 5:31–32). And if they are one flesh, and if the marriage is for real ... then it follows that everything that they have is held in common, whether good or evil. So the believer can boast of, and glory in, whatever Christ possesses, as though it were his or her own. And what-ever the believer has, Christ claims as His own.

Let us see how this works out, and see how it benefits us. Christ is full of grace, life, and salvation. The human soul is full of sin, death, and damna-tion. Now let faith come between them. Sin, death, and damnation will be Christ's. And grace, life, and salvation will be the believer's.

—Martin Luther, *The Liberty of a Christian*, 1520

6. How does the image of the flood in Noah's day remind us of the urgent need for people to have a relationship with Christ?

Who is one person in your life whom you could introduce to Jesus?

7. For many people, Jesus Christ is a lot like a bright orange life jacket. They know He is out there, but their sense of a need for Him is not very urgent. What does this passage teach about the death and resurrection of Jesus Christ?

Read 1 Peter 4:1–6

8. Peter calls us to keep one eye on the clock and be careful not to waste precious time that can be used for kingdom business. What are some of the things of the past that we are to leave behind?

Keep an Eye on the Clock!

It does not take long for a good high school basketball coach to teach his players to be aware of how much time is on the game clock. It is considered the ultimate embarrassment to be casually dribbling down the sidelines, winking at the cheerleaders, posing for the school yearbook photographers and to have the buzzer go off signaling the end of the quarter, half, or worst of all, the end of the game. Good coaches will tell the players over and over again, keep one eye on the clock.

In professional basketball the shot clock is ever present, reminding players that they had better get a shot off before the buzzer, or they forfeit the ball. If you watch a professional basketball player closely, you will see regular glances up to the shot clock to be sure they know exactly how much time is left. A player who is not attentive to this will start spending time on the bench, and eventually, could lose their place on the team. Watching the clock is that important!

If we don't leave these in our past, how might they cost us valuable time and energy?

9. Peter warns us that some nonbelievers will seek to draw us back into ungodly, time-wasting activities (vv. 4–5). What pressure tactics have you experienced from those who are bothered that you are living a new life in Christ?

What have you done to resist these pressures?

Celebrating and Being Celebrated

Take time as a group to pray together and celebrate God's great saving grace. Before you were born God loved you. Jesus came to this earth and gave His life for you, even when you were rebellious and had no desire to be His follower (Romans 5:8). The moment you believed in Him and received His forgiveness, the angels in heaven had a party (Luke 15:10). Since then, He has never let you go. Take time as a group to pray together and celebrate the gift of salvation you have received through Jesus Christ.

Serving and Being Served

Accountability is essential for building Christian community. Invite a group member to serve you by keeping you accountable in how you invest your time. Invite them to look at your calendar at the start of the month for the next three months. Let them encourage you to spend your time on things that will matter for eternity as well as point out where you might be wasting precious time that could be used more responsibly for the kingdom.

Understand, this business of building community means taking risks. Sometimes, you must invite another follower of Christ into a place where they can have an influence on your life.

Loving and Being Loved

The greatest gift of love we can give someone is to tell them about Jesus in a clear and relevant manner. Commit yourself to work on communicating your personal testimony. If you are not sure how to do this, there is a section in Willow Creek's Contagious Christian materials that will teach you to communicate your testimony. The next time your small group meets, invite members to practice telling how they came to faith in the safe and supportive context of your small group. Then pray for boldness for them to share their testimony with a seeker.

A Life of Service

I PETER 4:7–19

During my years of training in college I had a professor named Dr. Gilbert Bilezikian. I was a commuter, sat in the back of his class, and was usually the last one to walk into class and the first one to leave. I was doing youth ministry, and much of my time and energy were centered in the ministry I did with students.

Dr. B., as we called him, would often do things that were unconventional. Sometimes he would change hats on us, unannounced. He would stop being a college professor and become a prophet. One day Dr. B. came to class, and I could see he was carrying a heavy burden in his heart. Instead of standing behind the lectern, he sat on the table where we usually placed our papers and opened his Bible. He had no notes, no formal lecture, but he opened to Acts 2 and read it to the class. He spoke of the birth of the church and what this new community of believers looked like.

He reflected on what it must have been like for three thousand new believers to enter the church on the same day and all be baptized in the name of the Father, the Son, and the Holy Spirit. Then he challenged us to imagine what it must have taken to build these three thousand baby Christians into fully devoted followers of Christ. The vision of Acts 2 has become a core vision at Willow Creek Church. Read the record of what happened to these brand new believers:

> They devoted themselves to the apostles' teaching and to the fellowship, to the breaking of bread and to prayer. Everyone was filled with awe, and many wonders and miraculous signs were done by the apostles. All the believers were together and had everything in common. Selling

their possessions and goods, they gave to anyone as he had need. Every day they continued to meet together in the temple courts. They broke bread in their homes and ate together with glad and sincere hearts, praising God and enjoying the favor of all the people. And the Lord added to their number daily those who were being saved.

(Acts 2:42–47)

Making the Connection

1. As the picture of the early church unfolds in Acts 2, what aspects of this picture cause excitement and longing in your heart?

Can I Pray for You?

A woman from Willow Creek Church came up to me after a worship service and said, "Bill, God has moved me to begin to pray for you every day." I said, "I'm honored, thanks!" Then she said, "I want to pray intelligently for you. Could you tell me specifically what I can be praying for in the coming months?" I could count on one hand how many times I have been asked that! I had to stop and really think about it. It took me a little while, and then I gave her a small list of a few very specific needs in my life.

From time to time she will ask me how things are going in a very specific area of my life. I am amazed that she is so faithful and committed in her prayers for me.

As the years go by, I learn more and more that prayer is one of the truest tests of love. When someone is on their knees investing time in eternity praying on your behalf, they are offering one of the purest forms of service. As they plead and intercede on your behalf, they are lifting up one of the most unselfish acts of love a person could ever offer. Prayer is a radical act of service!

Read 1 Peter 4:7–19

2. What does Peter mean by the words *clear-minded* and *self-controlled* (v. 7)?

3. Respond to either one of these statements about prayer:

    I have so much to do that I must spend several hours in prayer before I am able to do it.

    —John Wesley

    Prayer is the key that unlocks all the storehouses of God's infinite grace and power: All that God is, and all that God has, is at the disposal of prayer.

    —R. A. Torrey

What If . . .

Most of us eat three meals a day. This means we have an average of twenty-one meals a week or ninety meals a month. What if every follower of Christ committed to invite someone new into their home once a month for a meal? What if we made a point of meeting someone new at church and simply asked them over for lunch? What if we established a habitual lifestyle of meeting new people and inviting them over for a meal?

What might happen? What new relationships might blossom? What kinds of hospitality might begin to infect the lives of God's people? How many people could be served and loved?

I only know one way to find out—give it a try!

4. What are some of the things that distract you and get in the way of your praying?

What has helped you pray more effectively?

5. Peter calls us to love each other deeply, and he states that "love covers over a multitude of sins" (v. 8). How is grace-filled, forgiving love a radical act of service?

6. Describe a time when you served another person by extending them forgiving love. What was the result of this service?

Describe a time when someone else served you by extending forgiving love. What was the result of their service in your relationship?

7. The word hospitality (v. 9) literally means "to take each other into your home." How is hospitality a powerful expression of service in our day and culture?

What are some practical ways we can express hospitality to each other?

8. Peter is clear that we all have a spiritual gift and that we are expected to use it in service to each other (vv. 10–11). What is one spiritual gift God has given you, and how are you using it to serve others?

What has helped you discover, sharpen, and learn how to use your spiritual gift?

Celebrating and Being Celebrated

Sometimes we celebrate good days, successful investments, and victories on the playing field of life. At other times we celebrate God's sustaining power to bring us through a difficult time. Peter teaches us that suffering and trials can bring glory to God and lead to rejoicing in our lives (4:12–19).

Invite a few members to tell about a time of struggle, trial, or suffering that God has brought them through. Pray for each other and celebrate God's power to bring us through even the darkest of times.

Serving and Being Served

There are many people who attend your church who hunger deeply to be in relationship with others. Some of these people are busy and have many friends, and others are lonely and have lots of time to spare. Some are outgoing and easy to notice, and others are very quiet and you have to look closely to notice they are there. For all of them, there is a need to connect, to relate, to build community.

Commit, as a group, to do some kind of activity, gathering, meal, or event where you can all invite and bring new people. Make a point of wandering around before and after church services and events at your church looking for new people to meet and invite to these events. As you walk around your church grounds, pray for the Holy Spirit to lead you to new people who need to experience community and the loving service of God's people. Then invite them to your next planned event. You will be amazed at what this act of service will mean to them!

Loving and Being Loved

Peter reminds us that one of the greatest expressions of service is forgiving each other. Take time this week to write in a journal, listing ways you have felt insulted or judged by others. Express your true thoughts and feelings. Then seek to forgive these offenses and pray for the offenders, confessing any bitterness, resentment, or anger you might hold in your heart. As you reflect, take time to read the following Bible passages: Matthew 5:23–24; Matthew 18:15–17 and 21–35; and Luke 17:3–4.

Before your group meets again, seek to extend forgiveness to these offenders in your heart. Remember the depth of God's forgiveness toward you. And, if need be, meet with someone to restore or reconcile a broken or fractured relationship.

A Life of Humility

I PETER 5:1–14

We don't live in a day and age where we see many shepherds and sheep wandering around fields near our homes. We live in a day of CPAs, computer programmers, investment bankers, and very, very few shepherds. However, in Peter's day, shepherding was a common occupation. It was so common that the Bible is filled with illustrations about sheep and shepherds. In the gospel of John, Jesus uses the image of a shepherd when He speaks of His own love and care for people:

> "I am the good shepherd. The good shepherd lays down his life for the sheep. The hired hand is not the shepherd who owns the sheep. So when he sees the wolf coming, he abandons the sheep and runs away. Then the wolf attacks the flock and scatters it. The man runs away because he is a hired hand and cares nothing for the sheep.
>
> "I am the good shepherd; I know my sheep and my sheep know me—just as the Father knows me and I know the Father—and I lay down my life for the sheep."
>
> (John 10:11–15)

Jesus establishes a dramatic contrast. On the one hand, there is the hired hand, who runs away and leaves the sheep vulnerable at the first sign of trouble. On the other hand, there is the shepherd who sees a wolf coming and charges forward for battle. If necessary, he will die, but he will never abandon his sheep.

Think about it, if you were a sheep, what kind of shepherd would you want watching over you when danger strikes?

The final chapter of 1 Peter uses the image of shepherds and sheep. Leaders in the church are called to shepherd God's flock with the right motives, attitudes, and commitments. Followers of Christ are called to be on the lookout for roaring lions who want to attack them and devour their faith and hope. In all of this, Peter wants us to know that victory is not only possible, it is promised for those who know the Chief Shepherd, Jesus Christ.

Making the Connection

1. What can happen to a church when its leaders are self-centered and motivated by greed?

Knowing and Being Known

Read I Peter 5:1–4

2. Peter speaks with clarity to all who are called to positions of leadership in the church—pastors, elders, small group leaders, and children's leaders, to name a few. In doing so, he states three vivid contrasts that every church leader must face. Write down each of these contrasts and discuss them:

    Contrast #1:

    Don't lead because . . .

But rather, lead because . . .

Contrast #2:
Don't lead motivated by . . .

But rather, lead because . . .

Contrast #3:
Don't lead by . . .

But rather, lead by . . .

The Good Shepherd

In his classic book, *A Shepherd Looks at Psalm 23* (Zondervan, 1970), Phillip Keller describes Jesus Christ, our best example of a Good Shepherd:

> He was the most balanced and perhaps the most beloved being ever to enter the society of men. Though born amid most disgusting surroundings, the member of a modest working family, He bore Himself always with great dignity and assurance. Though He enjoyed no special advantages as a child, either in education or employment, His entire philosophy and outlook on life were the highest standards of human conduct ever set before mankind....
>
> Not only was He gentle and tender and true but also righteous, stern as steel, and terribly tough on phony people.
>
> He was magnificent in His magnanimous spirit of forgiveness for fallen folk but a terror to those who indulged in double-talk or false pretenses.
>
> He came to set men free from their own sins, their own selves, their own fears. Those so liberated loved Him with fierce loyalty.
>
> It is this One who insists that He was the Good Shepherd, the understanding Shepherd, the concerned Shepherd who cares enough to seek out and save and restore lost men and women.

3. Contrast a well-shepherded flock with a poorly shepherded flock. What does a well-shepherded church look like?

4. Peter calls us to shepherd by being examples (v. 3), not by bossing them around. Describe one area where you need to grow in order to be a good example:

- How you relate to your friends
- How you worship
- How you serve within the church
- How you serve outside of the church
- How you pray
- How you study the Bible

Read 1 Peter 5:5–7

5. Peter speaks to every member of the church and says, "All of you, clothe yourselves with humility" (v. 5). In the world of fashion, there are clothes and there are accessories. What is the difference between clothing and accessories?

Why do you think Peter insists that we wear humility as our clothing and not as an accessory?

6. In Philippians 2:3, the apostle Paul makes a key statement that helps us define what humility is all about. Under the inspiration of the Holy Spirit, he tells us, "Do nothing out of selfish ambition or vain conceit, but in humility consider others better than yourselves." What might happen in one of the following areas of your life if you lived out this teaching?

   • In your workplace

   • In your home with your spouse or one of your children

   • In the grocery store

   • In your neighborhood

   • In your church

   • In a friendship

What is one practical way you are going to seek to live out this call to humility in the coming week?

Looking Back

One way to remain humble and battle against the poison of pride is to look back and remember where we have come from. Isaiah reminds us of the importance of this in Isaiah 51:1:

"Listen to me, you who pursue righteousness
and who seek the LORD:
Look to the rock from which you were cut
and to the quarry from which you were hewn."

In *Growing Strong in the Seasons of Life* (Zondervan, 1983), Charles Swindoll gives a brief survey of notable Bible characters whose pasts helped them remain humble as they served God in the present:

Let's not kid ourselves, even those who are extolled and admired have "holes" from which they were dug.

With Moses it was murder.
With Elijah it was deep depression.
With Peter it was public denial.
With Samson it was recurring lust.
With Thomas it was cynical doubting.
With Jacob it was deception.
With Rahab it was prostitution.
With Jephthah it was his illegitimate birth.

We all need help staying humble and avoiding the poison of pride as we live in community with other followers of Christ. Sometimes the best thing we can do is simply look back and remember the pit from which we were dug! When we see God's grace in our lives, we are moved to extend it to each other.

7. What is the difference between false humility and genuine humility?

Why is genuine humility irreplaceable for harmony and health among God's people?

8. "God opposes the proud but gives grace to the humble" (v. 5). Tell about a time when pride crept into your life and God brought you back down to earth.

What did you learn about humility through this experience?

Parting Advice

We are all familiar with parting advice. A junior high student is being dropped off to head to camp for a week. "Remember to take a shower at least once this week! Be sure to keep warm! Change your underwear! Watch out for poison ivy! Oh, and remember to have fun!"

A high school student gets her license and is ready to pull out of the driveway and head out for her first drive all alone. As she backs out she hears a loving, deeply concerned parent warning them, "Be sure to check your blind spot! Don't drive over the speed limit! The brake is on the left, don't be afraid to use it! Be home by 9:00! Remember, that's my car your driving!"

A college student is heading off to be on his own for four years. "Don't forget to hit the books. Don't hang out with the wrong crowd. Remember, this is an opportunity of a lifetime, make the most of it."

We all know the importance of parting advice, and so did Peter. At the close of this book we discover a series of very important warnings. These are final words written lovingly to followers of Christ who needed a word of encouragement. We should take these words just as seriously today as the early church took them two thousand years ago.

Read 1 Peter 5:8–14

9. In his parting words, Peter challenges us to be self-controlled as well as mentally and spiritually alert because there is a lion on the prowl who would love a succulent lamb dinner! What do you learn about your enemy, the Devil, in verses 8 and 9?

What is your "resistance strategy" for thwarting the Devil's tactics?

10. Most of us would prefer a life without pain and struggles. However, Peter is clear that God can bring good out of our times of suffering (vv. 10–11). How can God use times of suffering to strengthen His people?

How have you experienced this in your life?

Celebrating and Being Celebrated

We are all called to pray for those who are shepherds in the flock of God. Take time as a small group to pray in two very specific directions. First, lift up prayers of celebration and praise for those faithful shepherds who have cared for you and influenced your life of faith over the years. Second, pray for those God has called to shepherding ministry in your church. Pray for pastors, elders, small group leaders, youth leaders, children's teachers, and anyone called to a role of shepherding others. Use 1 Peter 5:1–4 as a guideline for your prayer.

Serving and Being Served

Paul calls us to, "Do nothing out of selfish ambition or vain conceit, but in humility consider others better than yourselves" (Philippians 2:3). Talk together as a group and choose one person in your church who has a ministry as a shepherd. This can be a small group leader, pastor, children's teacher, or any person who is effectively shepherding members of your church. Agree as a group on some tangible way that you can honor this person and affirm their ministry. This can be in the form of a small gift, words of affirmation, taking this person out for a meal, or any expression you feel would communicate your love and appreciation.

Loving and Being Loved

One of the greatest responsibilities in life is shepherding children. Every parent, grandparent, aunt, and uncle should seek to invest loving care in the lives of the children in their family. Talk as a group about various ways you can show love and care to the children in your extended family. Invite each group member to pick one child in their family that they will pray for and seek to shepherd over the coming months. Pray for each other in this important ministry over the coming months, and give occasional updates to group members.

Session One – A Life of Hope
I PETER 1:1–21

Question 1

Although many who read these words will never face persecution like the one described in the introduction to this session, we must remember that there are Christians around the world who do face intense persecution. They risk their reputations, resources, families, and even their lives in their commitment to be a follower of Christ. Allow yourself to imagine what it would be like to lose much of what you have simply because you are a Christian.

Questions 2–4

One treasure we all have as followers of Christ is the gift of a merciful God. We are invited into an intimate relationship with a God who is rich in mercy beyond our wildest dreams. Peter reminds these individuals of the fact that God could have treated them with justice. They could have received the penalty they deserved for their sins. But God has sovereignly chosen to be merciful. He is not obligated by anyone to be merciful. He has *chosen* to be merciful.

In this mercy He offers us another treasure: He has caused us to be born again. Not only do you have a merciful God, but in His mercy He caused a miracle to happen in your life: the miracle of spiritual rebirth. Because of God's love we can be born again into a relationship with a living Savior who gives us a living hope. That's the dynamic that separates Christianity from every other religion. When you're born again you have a living, dynamic relationship with God.

The essence of what Peter is saying is, "Some of you are in the catacombs right now, some of you live in tents, and you're losing hope. Some of you think your Savior is dead. But I'm here to tell you, He's not dead. He's alive and He's active and powerful! He's your hope! He will show you mercy when no one else will. He offers new life when you feel you can't go another day. He is the answer to all the heartache you face."

I believe God's message to us today has not changed. Some are holding on for dear life because of tragedies, problems, and difficulties in their lives. If this describes you, Peter would say, "Don't lose hope . . . because you have a living hope. You're in relationship with a living Savior."

Questions 5–7

In the midst of the trials of life, Peter is saying, "Keep your joy. Rejoice even though you have a few trials because when your faith is being tested by fire, it can become more precious than gold." In those days, a goldsmith would put a piece of gold ore in a crucible (a small metal cup). Then he would put the heat to it, and as that piece of ore would melt into liquid gold, the imperfections would rise to the surface. Then he would take a little tool, and he would scrape the imperfections off the surface of the gold. He would continue to put heat to it and keep skimming off those imperfections until he could look over and see his own face clearly reflected in the liquid gold. Then he knew it was pure gold.

In the same way, God will allow, from time to time, heat to be put into your life. Now granted, Satan wants the heat to destroy, disarm, discourage, and singe you. But God's intention in allowing that heat to come to your life through trials is to force your imperfections to the surface so the Holy Spirit can skim them away. When God looks at your life after He's put the heat to us and the Holy Spirit has skimmed away our imperfections, He sees His own reflection.

Questions 8–9

The apostle James said, "Faith without works is dead." Fully devoted followers of Christ are continually being transformed and shaped more and more into the image of Jesus. Peter is clear that our attitudes and actions will change when we come face-to-face with Jesus Christ, the risen Savior.

Question 10

Many people today are seeking to undermine the uniqueness of Jesus Christ and the Christian faith. Peter is crystal clear about who Jesus is and what He has done. Read 1 Peter 1:18–21 slowly and carefully. Jesus Christ is the sacrificial Lamb of God. It is through His blood that we can find salvation and new birth. Jesus is not one of many ways to God; He is the only way to the Father (John 14:6). Take time as a group and discuss the uniqueness of Jesus Christ as portrayed by Peter.

Session Two—A Life of Love
I PETER 1:22–2:10

Questions 2–3

The first priority for followers of Christ is getting right with God. Peter is clear that we need to be purified in God's sight before we can start influencing the lives of others. The Ten Commandments are an example of this. The first four of the commandments call us to get right with God. They are about loving God and growing in our commitment to Him. The next six commandments help us understand how we can love others. There is a clear order expressed in the commandments.

This is what Peter is saying. When we are right with God and walking in His light, then we are ready to love our brothers and sisters. Purity precedes quality relationships. The bridge to community is holiness.

In my own marriage I can chart on a graph the quality of our spiritual walk in relationship to how we get along as a couple. When we are both in tune with God and yielded to the Holy Spirit, our relationship is healthy and harmonious. When we are not growing as fully devoted followers of Christ, when we are neglecting our prayer lives and study of the Bible, we just don't get along as well. It shows very quickly and clearly.

Question 4

Our love is a response to the goodness and grace of God. He has loved us, forgiven us, given us new life, and promised an eternal inheritance that no one could ever take away. Our love for God and others grows out of a profound understanding of how deeply we are loved by God.

Question 5

God is in the business of building us up in love. However, there are many things that undermine and erode love among God's people. Take time to tell about real-life situations where you have seen love weakened. Reflect together on how you can be people who build up love and not those who tear it down.

Questions 7–8

Imagine you were a Christian in the first century who had been persecuted and driven away from your home, friends, and family. You would have felt like a scattered brick! The followers of Christ felt disorganized, disconnected, and discouraged. God spoke through Peter and said to His people . . . all of you together, brick by brick, make up a building for My glory, built on the foundation of Jesus Christ. Every one of you matters. Every one is important.

God is still building a spiritual house, and He needs every one of His people to take their place in His temple. Each one of us is essential. Each stone is in His plan. Each brick is strategic. We connect together to accomplish God's plan in this world. Therefore, don't chip, throw away, or discard any of God's bricks. Remember that every person matters to God, and they should matter just as much to us.

Questions 9–10

We must understand in Jewish history what it meant to be a priest. Some of the most honored men in the land were priests. They wore special garments and had a special calling. They were temple workers and they assisted in sacrifices. The priests had special access to various holy places and objects that the average Israelite couldn't get near. People were careful how they behaved around priests. They had a very special place.

In the face of all this Jewish history, Peter says that all followers of Christ are God's priests. This means we are honored in his sight. We have access to the Father through Jesus. We can enter the very holy place with confidence. This thought should have a powerful influence on how we see ourselves and others.

Session Three — A Life of Submission
I PETER 2:11–3:7

Questions 2–3

Peter looked at the early disciples and realized they had an image problem. Think about it. The followers of Christ to which Peter wrote were seen as vagabonds, refugees, maybe even gypsies. What would Christians today think about a group that had moved out to the desert and were on the run from the government? We need to realize that these early followers of Christ were considered suspect by mainstream culture.

What does Peter suggest to remedy this problem? Some might have thought the way to turn the tide of public opinion would have been through hiring a media consultant for the church. But Peter knew that a media blitz was not the answer. He knew that public opinion would only change through the face-to-face witness of these people. He reminded them to keep a joy-filled and hopeful attitude as they remembered their treasures more than their tragedies. Then Peter called them to holiness in God's sight and in the sight of the people. Finally, he called them to loving and harmonious relationships with each other and the seekers around them.

These opening verses become the umbrella for this whole session. Peter is saying, "First of all, you need to stay away from sin. People are watching you. Don't let them accuse you of sinful desires and actions." Never forget it: unbelievers watch followers of Christ. Next, Peter calls all Christ followers to live such good and holy lives that any accusation against them would be deemed ludicrous.

Questions 4–5

Peter says, "Submission! This is God's plan for us to let people know what followers of Christ are really all about." Now, we need to realize how serious of a commitment this was. Peter was talking about a commitment to submission that most of us can't imagine. It meant a submission to the Roman government, the very ones who had falsely accused Christians of burning Rome and were now out to destroy them. It meant submission of slaves to their masters. And it called for submission to spouses in marriage relationships.

Question 6

Followers of Christ should be model citizens. We should follow all laws (even traffic laws). We are called to follow all tax laws and not withhold one dime that we owe the government. This call to submission applies to building permits, zoning violations, and each and every area that we would like to justify away. We are under the command of God to obey the government.

This does not mean that we live with mindless compliance to everything we are told to do. If we disagree, there are ways, within the law, to voice our dissent. In a democracy we can campaign against bad leaders, pray for the hearts of leaders to change, and demonstrate and protest.

The Bible leaves room for us to resist and disobey only if the government makes a law that contradicts Scripture. As followers of Christ we know that God's authority is higher than governmental authority.

Question 7

When I talk to people who are having problems at work, and they are getting a little nasty and negative, I call them to obey this Scripture. They almost always say the same thing: "But you don't know my boss! If you did, you wouldn't ask me to do what he says." But then I ask, "Has the Word of God changed to accommodate your problems with your boss? I don't think so!"

Question 8

When we are feeling like being rebellious, when everything in us says, "Don't submit!"—these are the moments we have to turn our eyes to the cross. With every blow, beating, lashing, rejection, and word of mocking, Jesus cried out, "Your will be done! Your way! Your way! I submit to the Father's will over My own!"

No sour grapes. No complaining. No second guessing the will of the Father. We can never forget that it was through His submission that we are saved. Look to Jesus and allow His example to grow a submissive spirit in you.

Question 9

I can't count the number of times I have sat in my office with a couple who both refused to budge. They were at a stalemate. Neither would give an inch. "If you think I am going to say that I am sorry you are very wrong!" At this point I explain to the couple that there is no end to this until one of them takes the gloves off and decides to stop fighting.

One of them needs to submit. And I say, "I don't care which of you it is." All I know is that there is no room for healing until some submission breaks out in that relationship. I ask, "Are the things you are fighting about worth what you are about to risk? Are they worth your children, your marriage, everything you own, your friendships? Will one of you take off the gloves, walk to the center of the ring, and say, 'Let's do it your way this time'? Someone needs to break the cycle."

Session Four — A Life of Purpose
I PETER 3:8–4:6

Questions 2–3

Have you ever woken up on a sunny day and felt like there was a cloud over your life because you were "doing time with your conscience"? Have you ever arrived at church with joy and excitement, only to run into someone you have hurt or wronged? Have you ever dreaded a communion service because the Holy Spirit was reminding you that things in your life are not right?

Our conscience is like an internal judge that either approves our action, attitudes, and motives, or accuses us. The conscience has been called a window that lets in the light of God's truth. When we live in purity and our lives are in harmony with God's Word, the light of God floods into our heart. This leads to a sensitive, Christ-centered conscience. In other words, there is a righteous judge on the bench of our heart. When we do what is right in God's sight, there is an internal affirmation. However, when we stray from the path, there is conviction and a call to change.

There are also those who live with an unclean conscience. The window is dirty, and sometimes even covered over. In some cases, no light from God shines through, and our conscience is seared. The judge who sits on the bench of our heart has no sense of right or wrong. There is corruption. This judge no longer condemns sin but actually applauds it. There is no sense of right or wrong. Sadly, many people in our world live with a darkened conscience.

In Romans 1:18–32 there is a record of the process of the human conscience growing increasingly corrupt. Humanity runs from God. With each additional cycle of disobedience, hearts grow harder and harder. As the days pass, layers and layers of film form on the window of the heart. This leads to a conscience that no longer convicts of wrong and sometimes even affirms a sinful lifestyle.

When all is said and done, the bottom line is this, "Although they know God's righteous decree that those who do such things deserve death, they not only continue to do these very things but also approve of those who practice them" (Romans 1:32). Sadly, this describes the hearts and consciences of many people.

Question 4

Remember that Peter is writing to followers of Christ who are scattered because of persecution. The government was at war with the church, and Christians were on the run. It would have been easy for them to avoid all those who were not believers, to keep to themselves and to tell no one about their faith.

Yet Peter calls them to be ready, at all times, to tell others about Jesus Christ. He wants them to know that followers of Christ who refuse to tell others about what they have found, will live with a guilty conscience. On the other hand, when we gently and respectfully tell others about the love and person of Jesus, there is a joy and peace like nothing else this life offers.

In my life as a follower of Christ, the highest highs don't come from speaking to huge groups or building new facilities. My greatest joy comes from sitting face-to-face with a person who comes to know God's love, the sacrifice of Christ on the cross, and then confesses their sin and need for a Savior. Nothing puts more octane in my tank than watching a seeker enter a relationship with God through Christ—and I know the same will be true for you.

Questions 5–6

The book of Genesis shows the corruption of human hearts in the days of Noah. It seemed like almost everyone had a seared conscience and was running away from God. Judgment was on the horizon! Does this sound at all familiar? As fully devoted followers of Christ, we must be deeply committed to pray for those who are still seeking, yet have not found Christ.

Take time as a small group to talk openly about the people in your lives who do not yet know Christ. Commit yourselves to pray for one another as you seek to let these people know the reality of their condition apart from God and the gift God has offered them through Jesus Christ.

Question 7

There were many people on the Titanic who, in spite of warning bells, whistles, and pleas from the captain, elected to stay in the dining room to dance and eat rather than get in a lifeboat. They sat together reassuring each other that there was no way the Titanic would ever sink. All of us know how that story ended.

Most men and women who are still apart from God soothe each other with human speculations, vain philosophies, and false moral comparisons in an attempt to perpetuate their lifestyles with minimum interference from God, the Bible, the church, or anyone else. God tells us that one of the primary calls of the church and all followers of Christ is to give these people a wake-up call! We need to work like the crew of the Titanic, knocking on cabin doors, seeking to convince the passengers to come up on deck and get on a lifeboat. The good news for us is that there is room for everyone who will respond. There is no shortage of lifeboats. "Jesus Christ died for sins once for all, the righteous for the unrighteous, to bring you to God" (1 Peter 3:18).

Question 8

The theme of urgency and watching the clock runs throughout the Bible. Read the parable in Luke 12:16–21. Here is an example of someone who took their eye off the clock, and it cost him dearly! In Luke 12:35–40 there is additional teaching on the theme of keeping our eye on the clock. The apostle Paul was careful to remind us to make the most of our time.

Session Five — A Life of Service
I PETER 4:7–19

Question 1

Talk openly and freely of what the heart of God longs for the church, and let your hearts be captured by this vision.

Questions 2–4

Peter does not simply call us to prayer, but to a healthy and intelligent prayer life. It is easy to pray sloppy and careless prayers. As followers of Christ, when we pray, "Please be with me" we are forgetting that He already is with us! God has promised, "Lo, I am with you always, even to the end of the age!" "I will never leave you or forsake you!" "Can a nursing mother leave her child?" On and on God promises us that He is with us. This kind of prayer is careless and wasteful of precious prayer moments.

A better way to pray is, "Lord, make me more aware of your presence." We need to wake up to the reality of His presence. We need to tune in to it. Our prayers need to be clear-minded and consistent with the teaching of the Bible. Let's not waste time praying for what God has promised over and over again in His Word. Let's pray for the things that really matter.

God does not want us falling into the rut of meaningless and mindless repetitions, but to stay sharp and focused on those things that reflect the heart of God. It is too easy to get distracted by our busyness, the noise of life, full schedules, responsibilities, or our own selfish pursuits. We need to tune in to God and find a place where we can be quiet in His presence.

Finish your discussion on prayer by listening to each other express what has helped each person grow deeper in prayer. Learn from each other and encourage each other to continue growing as committed people of prayer.

Questions 5–6

Jesus called us over and over to love each other. He even said that this would be one of the primary ways the world will know that He is who He said He was. The apostle Paul said, "And now these three remain: faith, hope and love. But the greatest of these is love." The apostle John said that love in the church should be so strong that we would be willing to lay down our lives for each other. "This is how we know what love is: Jesus Christ laid down his life for us. And we ought to lay down our lives for our brothers." Love should mark the life of Christian community.

Peter says we should harbor and express a deep love for each other. The language in this passage is a picture of a runner near the end of a race who stretches for the tape at the finish line. Striving forward and pressing on . . . this is the image of love in a life committed to Christ.

One of the best definitions of love I have ever heard is this: Treat others the way Christ treats you. Think about that one for a while!

Love covers a multitude of sins. This is not to be taken literally. It does not mean that when we love someone we cover up their sins. It simply means a lot can go wrong in a church or relationship, but if there is a rock-solid foundation of love, healing can and will occur. When we are ruled by love, we will be committed to extend forgiveness to others even as Christ has extended forgiveness to us.

Question 8

Every one of us has received a special gift, a divine ability from God. We are called to use it to serve each other. Many in the church have discovered and begun to develop their spiritual gifts. Others still need to learn that they have a God-given endowment that is to be used to build up others. If you have group members who have still not discovered or begun to develop their gifts, you may want to encourage them to read the book *Networking*. If your church does not use a program for helping people discover their spiritual gifts, you may want to consider using the *Network* course.

Session Six—A Life of Humility
I PETER 5:1–14

Questions 2–4

One of God's highest callings in life is to challenge us to be shepherds of His people. One of our most fulfilling activities is the challenge of shepherding God's people. And, quite honestly, one of the most frustrating endeavors in life is to shepherd other people. If you have ever tried, you know exactly what I mean. This endeavor can bring the greatest joy and the deepest heartache.

When we see people moving toward full devotion to Christ and realize that we have had a small part of this miracle of God, we discover that this is what life is truly about. There are days when I fall on my knees and say, "Lord, You could bring me home today and I would be a completed man!" Being used as a shepherd to build into the lives of others is one of the greatest joys in my life! But I have also grieved when I have seen someone God has called me to shepherd begin to defect from the faith or live a halfhearted Christian life. Few things bring greater grief to the heart of a shepherd than seeing a person they love walking away from God.

When Peter calls us to shepherd God's people, we are called to get wrapped up in their lives, to give ourselves to them. This is never a light calling. It may be one of the greatest responsibilities we ever have. This is an investment in eternity.

Shepherds are called to analyze their motives. We should not enter a shepherding ministry under human obligation. Because when things get tough, we will cave. We will be like the hired servant who runs for the door when trials come. I plead with you shepherds—enter this ministry because you are called by God. We can never forget that the sheep can tell the condition of the heart of their shepherd. If a person is serving with no real excitement or interest in the lives of others, the sheep will see this a mile away.

Next we are warned to analyze our ambitions. Are we motivated by greed? If there is compensation for our shepherding ministry (and for some there is), be sure it does not become a business or a profession. Don't allow it to be a chore or a job to do because we get some kind of payoff. That payoff could be money, attention, or status, but none of these should motivate us. Shepherd others with a willing spirit and joy that wells up from within.

The third and final warning is to analyze our attitudes. Beware of a subtle air of superiority that can creep into the life of a leader. Exercise no unnecessary authority over the lives of others. Some people want to be in places of leadership so they can tell others what to do. They get a controlling and bossy spirit. We must never let this be our attitude. Rather, we must be servant-leaders who lead by our example in love.

In verse 4 Peter sums it all up by reminding us that the Chief Shepherd (Jesus) will reward us for our faithful service. We don't need human praise and selfish gain, but rather a willingness to love and shepherd God's people. We do this knowing that Jesus, our Good Shepherd, watches over us and will reward us according to our service.

Questions 5–8

Humility is absolutely essential for community among God's people. In Philippians the apostle Paul says, "Do nothing out of selfish ambition or vain conceit, but in humility consider others better than yourselves" (2:3). This is a passage that would yield much fruit if it were seared on the heart of every believer. Humility is a core attribute, a mark of the life of every follower of Christ.

Most of us own some kind of motorized vehicle. Within the engine are hundreds of metal parts that are constantly moving, banging against each other, and rubbing other metal parts. Your motor would disintegrate from heat and friction in a few moments if not for the presence of motor oil. This lubricant allows metal parts to function normally without building up excess heat. Oil reduces friction and drag. We can neglect many aspects of car care, but if we don't keep oil in the engine, a breakdown is on the horizon!

In the church there are hundreds and sometimes thousands of moving, semi-abrasive parts. These parts, the people, need to function together for the health of the church and the glory of God. Humility is the oil that reduces friction, heat buildup, and engine failure in the church.

Peter is telling the people that humility is like clothing to be worn by every believer. It can't be tagged on as an accessory. It is the primary garment we wear, and we need to wear it every day! It is part of the believer's wardrobe, like love, hope, and faith.

Question 9

There are at least six insights we can draw from this passage.

First, the Devil is real and personal. He exists. He is a spiritual being, often referred to with the personal pronoun. In this passage we are called to "resist *him*."

Second, Satan can cloak himself in whatever garb is needed for his work. In Eden he was a serpent. In 2 Corinthians 11:14 we learn that Satan can disguise himself as an angel of light. Followers of Christ need to know that Satan is a master deceiver, and we need to learn to identify his tactics, even when he is camouflaged and working undercover. Sometimes he mounts an all-out attack, a wide open assault. That's why he is called a roaring lion.

Third, he is the Christian's archenemy. He is our adversary. He stands against righteousness. This means that when we try to devote ourselves more fully to God, he will stand in the way.

Fourth, he prowls about. He is in perpetual motion. He never stops trying to cause trouble, deceive people, and destroy lives. He is in full-time business, and this ought to keep us on our toes.

Fifth, he is no respecter of persons. He is not fussy but will attack anyone who gives him an opening. No person is above the attacks of the Devil. Think about it. Read Matthew 4 and

Luke 4. Even Jesus is attacked by the enemy. If he would attack the only Son of God, he will attack anyone!

Sixth and finally, Satan's goal is destruction, even if he does not always succeed. He hungers and feeds on destroying the lives of believers and unbelievers alike. The idea that Satan is on the side of those who resist God is a lie, for he wants to destroy them as well. He has no friends.

WILLOW CREEK
RESOURCES

Vision,   Training,   Resources,

This resource was created to serve you and to help you in building a local church that prevails! It is just one of many Willow Creek Resources copublished by the Willow Creek Association and Zondervan.

Since 1992, the Willow Creek Association (WCA) has been linking like-minded, action-oriented churches with each other and with strategic vision, training, and resources. Now a worldwide network of over five thousand churches from more than eighty denominations, the WCA works to equip Member Churches and others with the tools needed to build prevailing churches. Our desire is to inspire, equip, and encourage Christian leaders to build biblically functioning churches that reach increasing numbers of unchurched people, not just with innovations from Willow Creek Community Church in South Barrington, Illinois, but from any church in the world that has experienced God-given breakthroughs.

Willow Creek Conferences

In the past year, more than 65,000 local church leaders, staff, and volunteers—from WCA Member Churches and others—attended one of our conferences or training events.

Conferences offered on the Willow Creek campus in South Barrington, Illinois, include:

Prevailing Church Conference—Foundational training for staff and volunteers working to build a prevailing local church; offered twice each year.

Prevailing Church Workshops—More than fifty workshops cover seven topic areas that represent key characteristics of a prevailing church; offered twice each year.

Promiseland Conference—Children's ministries; infant through fifth grade.

Prevailing Youth Ministries Conference—Junior and senior high ministries.

Arts Conference—Vision and training for Christian artists using their gifts in the ministries of local churches.

Leadership Summit—Envisioning and equipping Christians with leadership gifts and responsibilities; broadcast live via satellite to sixteen cities.

Contagious Evangelism Conference—Encouragement and training for churches and church leaders who want to be strategic in reaching lost people for Christ.

Small Groups Conference—Exploring how small groups can play a key role in developing authentic Christian community that leads to spiritual transformation.

Prevailing Church Regional Workshops

Each year the WCA team leads seven, two-day training events in cities across the United States. Workshops are offered in topic areas including leadership, next-generation ministries, small groups, arts and worship, evangelism, spiritual gifts, financial stewardship, and spiritual formation. These events make quality training more accessible and affordable to larger groups of staff and volunteers.

Willow Creek Resources

Churches can look to Willow Creek Resources for a trusted channel of ministry tools in areas of leadership, evangelism, spiritual gifts, small groups, drama, contemporary music, financial stewardship, spiritual transformation, and more. For ordering information, call 800-570-9812 or visit www.willowcreek.com.

WCA Membership

Membership in the Willow Creek Association as well as attendance at WCA Conferences is for churches, ministries, and leaders who hold to a historic, orthodox understanding of biblical Christianity. The annual church membership fee of $249 provides discounts for your entire team on all conferences and Willow Creek Resources, networking opportunities with other outreach-oriented churches, a bimonthly newsletter, a subscription to *Defining Moments* monthly audio journal, and more.

WillowNet (www.willowcreek.com)

This internet service provides you with access to hundreds of Willow Creek messages, drama scripts, songs, videos, and multimedia suggestions. The system allows you to sort through these elements and download them for a fee.

Our website also provides detailed information on the Willow Creek Association, Willow Creek Community Church, WCA Membership, conferences, training events, resources, and more.

Willow Creek Association
P.O. Box 3188
Barrington, IL 60011-3188
Phone: 800-570-9812
Fax: 888-922-0035
Web: www.willowcreek.com

Continue building your new community!

New Community Series

Bill Hybels and John Ortberg

with Kevin and Sherry Harney

If you appreciate not having to choose between Bible study and building community, then you'll want to explore all eight New Community Bible study guides. Delve deeply into Scripture in a way that strengthens relationships. Challenging questions will encourage your group members to reflect not only on Scripture but also on the old idea of community done in a new, culturally relevant way.

Each guide contains six transforming sessions—filled with prayer, insight, intimacy, and action—to help your small group members line up their lives and relationships more closely with the Bible's model for the church.

James: **Live Wisely**	0-310-22767-4
1 Peter: **Stand Strong**	0-310-22773-9
Romans: **Find Freedom**	0-310-22765-8
Philippians: **Run the Race**	0-310-22766-6
Colossians: **Discover the New You**	0-310-22769-0
1 John: **Love Each Other**	0-310-22768-2
Exodus: **Journey Toward God**	0-310-22771-2
Acts: **Build Community**	0-310-22770-4

*Look for New Community at
your local Christian bookstore.*

WILLOW CREEK

RESOURCES

www.willowcreek.org

ZONDERVAN™

GRAND RAPIDS, MICHIGAN 49530

www.zondervan.com

Bring your group to a deeper level of interaction!
InterActions Series
Bill Hybels

Help your small-group members help each other develop into fully devoted followers of Christ. InterActions discussion guides ask for a deeper level of sharing, creating lines of accountability between individuals and moving your group into action. Each book presents six thought-provoking sessions specifically designed to build on the dynamics and interplay of small groups.

Essential Christianity: Practical Steps for Spiritual Growth	0-310-21317-7
Getting a Grip: Finding Balance in Your Daily Life	0-310-21318-5
Overcoming: Applying God's Power Where You Need It Most	0-310-21717-2
Serving Lessons: Putting God and Others First	0-310-21315-0
Authenticity: Being Honest with God and Others	0-310-20674-X
Commitment: Developing Deeper Devotion to Christ	0-310-20683-9
Community: Building Relationships Within God's Family	0-310-20677-4
Evangelism: Becoming Stronger Salt and Brighter Light	0-310-20678-2
Lessons on Love: Following Christ's Example	0-310-20680-4
Marriage: Building Real Intimacy	0-310-20675-8.
Parenthood: Rising to the Challenge of a Lifetime	0-310-20676-6
The Real You: Discovering Your Identity in Christ	0-310-20682-0
Character: Reclaiming Six Endangered Qualities	0-310-21716-4
Freedom: Breaking the Chains that Bind You	0-310-21717-2
Fruit of the Spirit: Living the Supernatural Life	0-310-21315-0
Jesus: Seeing Him More Clearly	0-310-21316-9
Prayer: Opening Your Heart to God	0-310-21714-8
Psalms: Deepening Your Relationship with God	0-310-21318-5
Transformation: Letting God Change You from the Inside Out	0-310-21317-7
Transparency: Discovering the Rewards of Truth-Telling	0-310-21715-6

Look for Interactions at your local Christian bookstore.

WILLOW CREEK
RESOURCES

www.willowcreek.org

ZONDERVAN™

GRAND RAPIDS, MICHIGAN 49530
www.zondervan.com

Walk with God Together
Walking With God Series
Don Cousins and Judson Poling

This series of six guides (and two leader's guides) provides a solid, biblical program of study for all of the small groups in your church. The Walking With God Series is designed to help lead new and young believers into a deeper personal intimacy with God, while at the same time building a strong foundation in the faith for all believers, regardless of their level of maturity. These guides are also appropriate for individual study. Titles in the series are:

Friendship with God: Developing Intimacy with God	0-310-59143-0
The Incomparable Jesus: Experiencing the Power of Christ	0-310-59153-8
"Follow Me!": Walking with Jesus in Everyday Life	0-310-59163-5
Leader's Guide 1 (covers these first three books)	0-310-59203-8
Discovering Your Church: Becoming Part of God's New Community	0-310-59173-2
Building Your Church: Using Your Gifts, Time, and Resources	0-310-59183-X
Impacting Your World: Becoming a Person of Influence	0-310-59193-7
Leader's Guide 2 (covers these last three books)	0-310-59213-5
Also available: *Walking With God Journal*	0-310-91642-9

Look for the Walking With God Series
at your local Christian bookstore.

WILLOW CREEK
RESOURCES

www.willowcreek.org

ZONDERVAN™

GRAND RAPIDS, MICHIGAN 49530
www.zondervan.com

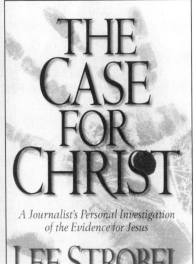

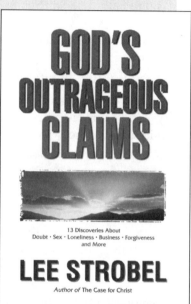

The Life You've Always Wanted

John Ortberg

Foreword by Bill Hybels

"John Ortberg takes Jesus' call to abundant living seriously, joyfully, and realistically. He believes human transformation is genuinely possible, and he describes its process in sane and practical ways."

—**Richard Foster,** author, *Celebration of Discipline* and *Prayer: Finding the Heart's True Home*

Willow Creek teaching pastor John Ortberg calls us to the dynamic heartbeat of Christianity—God's power to bring change and growth—and shows us how we can attain it. Salvation without change was unheard-of among Christians of other days, he says, so why has the church today reduced faith to mere spiritual "fire insurance" that omits the best part of being a Christian?

As with a marathon runner, the secret of the Christian life lies not in trying harder, but in training consistently. *The Life You've Always Wanted* outlines seven spiritual disciplines and offers a road map toward true transformation, compelling because it starts out not with ourselves but with the object of our journey—Jesus Christ. Ortberg takes spiritual disciplines out of the monastery and onto Main Street, and leads readers to transformation and true intimacy with God.

Hardcover: 0-310-21214-6
Softcover: 0-310-22699-6

Look for The Life You've Always Wanted *at your local bookstore.*

www.willowcreek.org

GRAND RAPIDS, MICHIGAN 49530

www.zondervan.com

We want to hear from you. Please send your comments about this book to us in care of the address below. Thank you.

ZONDERVAN™

GRAND RAPIDS, MICHIGAN 49530

www.zondervan.com